Down in Louisiana

Down in Louisiana

Traditional Song Adapted by Johnette Downing
Illustrated by Deborah Ousley Kadair

PELICAN PUBLISHING COMPANY
GRETNA 2009

For Dad, who shared with me his love of books — J. D.

To my first teacher and my forever friend, my sister Christy.
Thanks for encouraging me to illustrate. You always see the best in me! — D. O. K

First printing, May 2007
Second printing, April 2009

The word "Pelican" and the depiction of a pelican
are trademarks of Pelican Publishing Company, Inc.,
and are registered in the U.S. Patent and Trademark Office.

Library of Congress Cataloging-in-Publication Data

Downing, Johnette.
  Down in Louisiana : traditional song / adapted by Johnette Downing ; illustrated by Deborah Ousley Kadair.
     p. cm.
  Summary: A variety of Louisiana animals pursuing their daily activities introduce the numbers one through ten. Includes a page of music.
  ISBN 978-1-58980-451-7 (hardcover : alk. paper)
  1. Nursery rhymes. 2. Children's poetry. [1. Nursery rhymes. 2. Animals--Poetry. 3. Louisiana--Poetry. 4. Counting.] I. Kadair, Deborah Ousley, ill. II. Title.
  PZ8.3.D75397Dow 2007
  811'.6--dc22
                       2006036283

Printed in Singapore
Published by Pelican Publishing Company, Inc.
1000 Burmaster Street, Gretna, Louisiana 70053

Down in Louisiana

Down in Louisiana in the wind and the sun
Lived a mother pelican and her pelican one.
"Fly," said the mother; "We fly," said the one,
And they flew all day in the wind and the sun.

Down in Louisiana near the ol' bayou
Lived a mother armadillo and her armadillos two.
"Dig," said the mother; "We dig," said the two,
And they dug all day near the ol' bayou.

Down in Louisiana in a cypress tree
Lived a mother black bear and her black bears three.
"Climb," said the mother; "We climb," said the three,
And they climbed all day in a cypress tree.

Down in Louisiana near the basin floor
Lived an alligator gar and her little gars four.
"Swim," said the mother; "We swim," said the four,
And they swam all day near the basin floor.

Down in Louisiana where the wetlands thrive
Lived a mother Catahoula and her Catahoulas five.
"Bark," said the mother; "We bark," said the five,
And they barked all day where the wetlands thrive.

Down in Louisiana where the bullfrog kicks
Lived a mother nutria and her nutrias six.
"Eat," said the mother; "We eat," said the six,
And they ate all day where the bullfrog kicks.

Down in Louisiana in a live oak haven
Lived a mother possum and her possums seven.
"Sleep," said the mother; "We sleep," said the seven,
And they slept all day in a live oak haven.

Down in Louisiana in a pond by the gate
Lived a mother crawfish and her crawfish eight.
"Snap," said the mother; "We snap," said the eight,
And they snapped all day in a pond by the gate.

Down in Louisiana in a marsh so fine
Lived a mother alligator and her alligators nine.
"Sun," said the mother; "We sun," said the nine,
And they sunned all day in a marsh so fine.

Down in Louisiana in a swamp with their kin
Lived a mother mosquito and her skeeters ten.
"Buzz," said the mother; "We buzz," said the ten,
And they buzzed all day in a swamp with their kin.

Down in Louisiana

Traditional Song Adapted by Johnette Downing

Down in Lou - i - si - an - a in the wind and the sun lived a moth - er pel - i -

can and her pel - i - can one. "Fly," said the moth - er; "We fly," said the

one, and they flew al - l d - ay in the wind and the sun.